MOSES IN THE BULRUSHES

Retold by Ronne Randall
Illustrated by Sara Sliwinska

Flying Frog Publishing

Long years ago, the children of Israel lived in a land called Canaan. But a time came when there was not enough food in Canaan to feed all the people, so the Israelites went to Egypt, where food was plentiful.

The Egyptians welcomed the Israelites, and so did their king, who was called Pharaoh.

Flying Frog Publishing, Inc.
Auburn, Maine 04210 U.S.A.
Copyright © 1996 Flying Frog Publishing, Inc.
Printed in Canada

When the old king died, a new Pharaoh came to the throne.

This new Pharaoh was afraid that the Israelites might rise up against him. So he took away their freedom and made them slaves.

The Israelites worked hard in the Egyptians' fields, and they built great cities for Pharaoh. They suffered terribly, for their Egyptian masters treated them harshly.

But still the Israelites grew in number, and Pharaoh grew even more afraid of them.

At last Pharaoh made a very cruel law. He said that every son born to the Israelites must be put to death. This way, he thought, he would get rid of the Israelites once and for all.

Now, at that time, there was an Israelite woman named Yocheved who had a baby boy. Although the law said he must die, she decided to try to save her baby's life. She hid him away where Pharaoh's soldiers would not find him.

When the baby was three months old, Yocheved gathered some bulrushes, the tall reeds that grew by the river Nile. She wove them into a basket that was just big enough to hold her baby.

Yocheved brushed the basket with tar, so no water could get in. Then she wrapped her baby in warm blankets, put him in the basket, and took him down to the river. Her daughter Miriam went with her.

Yocheved left the basket in the reeds by the riverbank, and told Miriam to stay and watch her baby brother.

"See what happens to him, and come and tell me," said Yocheved. So Miriam stayed and watched.

Every day, Pharaoh's daughter came with her handmaidens to bathe in the Nile. When she came to the river that day, she saw the little basket floating among the bulrushes.

The princess wondered what was in the basket, and she asked one of her maidens to bring it to her.

When she saw the tiny baby, Pharaoh's daughter was filled with tenderness. "This must be an Israelite baby," she said. "How beautiful he is!"

She decided to call him Moses, which means "to draw out," for he had been drawn out of the water.

All at once Miriam stepped out from her hiding place. "Your Highness," she said to the princess, "I know an Israelite woman who can look after the baby for you. Shall I get her?"

"Yes, " said Pharaoh's daughter.

Miriam rushed home and got her mother, and brought her to the princess.

"Please take this child home and look after him till he is older," the princess said to Yocheved. "I will pay you well."

Yocheved was filled with joy, but she did not give away her secret. She simply said, "I will do as you ask," and took Moses from the princess.

So Moses was cared for by his own mother until he was seven years old.

Then he went to the palace to live with Pharaoh's daughter. She loved him and treated him as if he were her own son.

But Moses always knew that Yocheved was his real mother, and that he was an Israelite. And when he grew up, he became a great leader who brought his people out of slavery in Egypt and led them to freedom in the land of Canaan.